Published by Creative Education
P.O. Box 227, Mankato, Minnesota 56002
Creative Education is an imprint of
The Creative Company
www.thecreativecompany.us

Design by The Design Lab
Production by Chelsey Luther
Art direction by Rita Marshall
Printed in the United States of America

Photographs by 123rf (Paul Hampton), Biosphoto
(J.-L. Klein & M.-L. Hubert), Corbis (Tom Brakefield,
Frans Lanting), Dreamstime (Stef Bennett, Gillmalo,
Christopher Moncrieff), Getty Images (Steve Winter),
iStockphoto (Paula Connelly), National Geographic
(SA TEAM/FOTO NATURA/MINDEN PIC), Photo
Researchers (Mark Newman, Millard H. Sharp),
Shutterstock (Ammit)

Library of Congress Cataloging-in-Publication Data
Bodden, Valerie.
Jaguars / by Valerie Bodden.
p. cm. — (Amazing animals)
Summary: A basic exploration of the appearance,
behavior, and habitat of jaguars, the largest cats of
the Americas. Also included is a story from folklore
explaining why jaguars have blurry spots.
Includes bibliographical references and index.
ISBN 978-1-60818-086-8
1. Jaguar—Juvenile literature. I. Title.
QL737.C23B6426 2013
599.75'5—dc23   2011050284

CPSIA: 040913 PO1675

9 8 7 6 5 4 3 2

AMAZING ANIMALS

JAGUARS

BY VALERIE BODDEN

CREATIVE EDUCATION

Jaguars are the third-largest cats in the world. Only lions and tigers are bigger. The word jaguar means "beast that kills with one leap."

The jaguar is the biggest cat in the Americas

Jaguars sharpen their claws by scratching tree trunks

Most jaguars have orange, yellow, or tan fur with black rings called rosettes (*roh-ZETZ*). The rosettes have lines and spots inside them. Some jaguars have black fur with black rosettes. Jaguars have sharp teeth and claws. Their feet are padded. This helps them sneak up on **prey**.

prey animals that are killed and eaten by other animals

Male jaguars can weigh up to 220 pounds (100 kg). Females are generally smaller. Jaguars have long bodies. Their tails can be almost three feet (0.9 m) long. Jaguars are good leapers. They can spring 20 feet (6 m) in one jump!

Jaguars are about 2.5 feet (0.8 m) ꞇꞓꞁꞁ

Jaguars in zoos may live in areas that look like forests

Jaguars live in Mexico, Central America, and South America. Most jaguars live in **rainforests** or **swamps**. But some live in hot, sandy deserts or dry, grassy spaces.

rainforests forests with many trees and lots of rain

swamps wet, muddy areas with a lot of plants

Among the jaguar's favorite prey is the capybara (*kap-uh-BAR-uh*). Capybaras look like big guinea pigs. Jaguars also eat monkeys, deer, and even big fish!

A jaguar's sharp teeth cut through meat

*Jaguar cubs cannot see
when they are first born*

Female jaguars have one to four babies, or cubs, at a time. The cubs weigh less than two pounds (0.9 kg) when they are born. They stay with their mother for two years. Jaguars have to watch out for human hunters, **caimans**, and big snakes called anacondas. Wild jaguars can live 12 to 15 years.

caimans animals in the same family as alligators

A jaguar's roar sounds like a deep cough

Adult jaguars live alone. Each jaguar has its own **territory**. Jaguars spend much of their time walking around their territory. They roar and spread their scent to keep other jaguars away.

territory a space that is the home of one animal

During the day, jaguars often rest. Sometimes they like to swim. Jaguars do their best hunting at night. They can see very well in the dark.

Jaguars are better swimmers than most other cats

People have hunted jaguars and cut down the rainforests where they live. But many jaguars are guarded in wildlife parks. Some people go to the parks to look at wild jaguars. Others watch jaguars in zoos. It can be exciting to see these big cats eat, swim, and roar!

Young jaguars at zoos like to climb and play

A Jaguar Story

Why do the jaguar's spots look unclear, or blurry? People in South America used to tell a story about this. They said that a sun **god** painted all the animals. He used coal to paint spots on the jaguar. But the jaguar ran away to show off his new spots too soon. The spots spread out when he ran. And from then on, jaguars have had spots that look blurry!

god a being thought to have special powers and control over the world

Read More

Cole, Melissa, Tom Leeson, and Pat Leeson. *Jaguars and Leopards*. San Diego: Blackbirch Press, 2002.

Huggins-Cooper, Lynn. *Big Cats*. North Mankato, Minn.: Smart Apple Media, 2006.

Riggs, Kate. *Rainforests*. Mankato, Minn.: Creative Education, 2010.

Web Sites

National Geographic Kids Creature Features: Jaguars
http://kids.nationalgeographic.com/kids/animals/creaturefeature/jaguars/
This site has jaguar facts, pictures, and videos.

San Diego Zoo Kids: Jaguar
http://kids.sandiegozoo.org/animals/mammals/jaguar
This site has jaguar pictures and information.

Index